MAD LIBS®

Napoleon Dynamite™

W9-AEB-545

By Roger Price and Leonard Stern

PSS!

PRICE STERN SLOAN

PRICE STERN SLOAN
Published by the Penguin Group
Penguin Group (USA) Inc., 375 Hudson Street,
New York, New York 10014, U.S.A.
Penguin Group (Canada), 90 Eglinton Avenue East, Suite 700
Toronto, Ontario, Canada M4P 2Y3
(a division of Pearson Penguin Canada Inc.)
Penguin Books Ltd, 80 Strand, London WC2R 0RL, England
Penguin Ireland, 25 St Stephen's Green, Dublin 2, Ireland
(a division of Penguin Books Ltd)
Penguin Group (Australia), 250 Camberwell Road,
Camberwell, Victoria 3124, Australia
(a division of Pearson Australia Group Pty Ltd)
Penguin Books India Pvt Ltd, 11 Community Centre,
Panchsheel Park, New Delhi - 110 017, India
Penguin Group (NZ), Cnr Airborne and Rosedale Roads,
Albany, Auckland 1310, New Zealand
(a division of Pearson New Zealand Ltd)
Penguin Books (South Africa) (Pty) Ltd, 24 Sturdee Avenue,
Rosebank, Johannesburg 2196, South Africa

Penguin Books Ltd, Registered Offices:
80 Strand, London WC2R 0RL, England

Mad Libs format copyright © 2005 by Price Stern Sloan.

© 2005 Twentieth Century Fox Film Corporation and Paramount Pictures Corporation.
All Rights Reserved.

Published by Price Stern Sloan,
a division of Penguin Young Readers Group,
345 Hudson Street, New York, New York 10014.

Printed in the United States of America. No part of this publication may be
reproduced, stored in any retrieval system, or transmitted, in any form or by any
means, electronic, mechanical, photocopying, or otherwise, without the prior written
permission of the publisher.

ISBN 0-8431-2011-8

1 3 5 7 9 10 8 6 4 2

PSS! and *MAD LIBS* are registered trademarks of Penguin Group (USA) Inc.

MAD LIBS®
INSTRUCTIONS

MAD LIBS® is a game for people who don't like games!
It can be played by one, two, three, four, or forty.

• RIDICULOUSLY SIMPLE DIRECTIONS

In this tablet you will find stories containing blank spaces where words are left out. One player, the **READER**, selects one of these stories. The **READER** does not tell anyone what the story is about. Instead, he/she asks the other players, the **WRITERS**, to give him/her words. These words are used to fill in the blank spaces in the story.

• TO PLAY

The **READER** asks each **WRITER** in turn to call out a word—an adjective or a noun or whatever the space calls for—and uses them to fill in the blank spaces in the story. The result is a **MAD LIBS®** game.

When the **READER** then reads the completed **MAD LIBS®** game to the other players, they will discover that they have written a story that is fantastic, screamingly funny, shocking, silly, crazy, or just plain dumb—depending upon which words each **WRITER** called out.

• EXAMPLE (*Before* and *After*)

"_____!" he said _____
              EXCLAMATION   ADVERB

as he jumped into his convertible _____ and
                                          NOUN

drove off with his _____ wife.
                          ADJECTIVE

"_____*Ouch!*_____!" he said _____*stupidly*_____
         EXCLAMATION   ADVERB

as he jumped into his convertible _____*cat*_____ and
                                          NOUN

drove off with his _____*brave*_____ wife.
                          ADJECTIVE

MAD LIBS®
QUICK REVIEW

In case you have forgotten what adjectives, adverbs, nouns, and verbs are, here is a quick review:

An **ADJECTIVE** describes something or somebody. *Lumpy, soft, ugly, messy,* and *short* are adjectives.

An **ADVERB** tells how something is done. It modifies a verb and usually ends in "ly." *Modestly, stupidly, greedily,* and *carefully* are adverbs.

A **NOUN** is the name of a person, place, or thing. *Sidewalk, umbrella, bridle, bathtub,* and *nose* are nouns.

A **VERB** is an action word. *Run, pitch, jump,* and *swim* are verbs. Put the verbs in past tense if the directions say PAST TENSE. *Ran, pitched, jumped,* and *swam* are verbs in the past tense.

When we ask for **A PLACE**, we mean any sort of place: a country or city *(Spain, Cleveland)* or a room *(bathroom, kitchen).*

An **EXCLAMATION** or **SILLY WORD** is any sort of funny sound, gasp, grunt, or outcry, like *Wow!, Ouch!, Whomp!, Ick!,* and *Gadzooks!*

When we ask for specific words, like a **NUMBER**, a **COLOR**, an **ANIMAL**, or a **PART OF THE BODY**, we mean a word that is one of those things, like *seven, blue, horse,* or *head.*

When we ask for a **PLURAL**, it means more than one. For example, *cat* pluralized is *cats.*

MAD LIBS® is fun to play with friends, but you can also play it by yourself! To begin with, DO NOT look at the story on the page below. Fill in the blanks on this page with the words called for. Then, using the words you have selected, fill in the blank spaces in the story.

Now you've created your own hilarious MAD LIBS® game!

MEET NAPOLEON DYNAMITE

NOUN _____

PERSON IN ROOM (MALE)_____

NOUN _____

SAME PERSON _____

VERB ENDING IN "ING" _____

ADJECTIVE_____

NOUN _____

ADJECTIVE_____

NOUN _____

SILLY WORD_____

NOUN _____

NOUN _____

SAME PERSON _____

ADJECTIVE_____

PLURAL NOUN _____

MAD LIBS
MEET NAPOLEON DYNAMITE

Napoleon needs help choosing people for his _____ club,
                                                    NOUN

so he's given us this application filled out by _____ .
                                                PERSON IN ROOM (MALE)

Let's review it and see if he's our kind of _____:
                                                    NOUN

1.   Q: What's your campaign slogan?

     A: "Free _____."
              SAME PERSON

2.   Q: What are your skills?

     A: _____, _____ arts, and
        VERB ENDING IN "ING"   ADJECTIVE

     _____ riding.
             NOUN

3.   Q: What would you say is your most _____ trait?
                                              ADJECTIVE

     A: My sense of _____.
                          NOUN

4.   Q: What's your favorite mythical creature?

     A: The _____. It's half-_____ and
              SILLY WORD   NOUN

     half-_____.
               NOUN

Well it's obvious that _____ is a flippin'
                              SAME PERSON

_____ candidate. I think he'll become one of our best
     ADJECTIVE

_____.
     PLURAL NOUN

From NAPOLEON DYNAMITE™ MAD LIBS® © 2005 Twentieth Century Fox Film Corporation
and Paramount Pictures Corporation. All Rights Reserved. Published by Price Stern Sloan,
a division of Penguin Young Readers Group, 345 Hudson Street, New York, New York 10014.

MAD LIBS® is fun to play with friends, but you can also play it by yourself! To begin with, DO NOT look at the story on the page below. Fill in the blanks on this page with the words called for. Then, using the words you have selected, fill in the blank spaces in the story.

Now you've created your own hilarious MAD LIBS® game!

WANNA PLAY ME?

PLURAL NOUN _____

ADJECTIVE _____

NUMBER _____

PERSON IN ROOM (MALE) _____

NOUN _____

PART OF THE BODY _____

NOUN _____

NOUN _____

NOUN _____

NOUN _____

ADJECTIVE _____

NOUN _____

NOUN _____

MAD LIBS
WANNA PLAY ME?

I was nervous, literally shaking in my _____,

PLURAL NOUN

as I approached the school's tetherball grounds. Throngs of

_____ fans were milling around; _____,

ADJECTIVE   NUMBER

to be exact. And they cheered, "Good luck, _____!

PERSON IN ROOM (MALE)

Break a/an _____!" Slowly, I approached my opponent

NOUN

and shook his _____. We took our positions. *Bam!* I

PART OF THE BODY

slapped the _____ around the pole faster than a

NOUN

speeding _____. *Bam!* He slapped it back, eyeing me

NOUN

like a vicious _____. I dug deep within my inner

NOUN

_____ for strength, and *bam!* I won the _____

NOUN   ADJECTIVE

game! It was probably the best match I ever played, and since that

day I've been known around our _____ as "The _____

NOUN   NOUN

Master."

From NAPOLEON DYNAMITE™ MAD LIBS® © 2005 Twentieth Century Fox Film Corporation
and Paramount Pictures Corporation. All Rights Reserved. Published by Price Stern Sloan,
a division of Penguin Young Readers Group, 345 Hudson Street, New York, New York 10014.

MAD LIBS® is fun to play with friends, but you can also play it by yourself! To begin with, DO NOT look at the story on the page below. Fill in the blanks on this page with the words called for. Then, using the words you have selected, fill in the blank spaces in the story.

Now you've created your own hilarious MAD LIBS® game!

THE NEW KID

NOUN _____

NOUN _____

NOUN _____

NOUN _____

ADJECTIVE _____

NOUN _____

NOUN _____

ADVERB _____

PLURAL NOUN _____

NOUN _____

NOUN _____

MAD LIBS
THE NEW KID

It sure is tough being the new _____ in town—especially
<u>NOUN</u>

at school. The first day, I got lost on the way to _____
<u>NOUN</u>

class. Then I forgot the combination to my _____ and
<u>NOUN</u>

had to ask the school _____ to open it for me. Next,
<u>NOUN</u>

some real _____-looking guys tried to steal my lunch
<u>ADJECTIVE</u>

_____. I was so frightened, I stared at them like a/an
<u>NOUN</u>

_____ in headlights. Then, _____, a boy
<u>NOUN</u>   <u>ADVERB</u>

rushed over and screamed in a Spanish accent. Amazingly, they ran

like scared _____. "Pedro offers you his protection,"
<u>PLURAL NOUN</u>

the boy said as he handed me a boondoggle _____
<u>NOUN</u>

and galloped off like a heroic _____ into the sunset.
<u>NOUN</u>

From NAPOLEON DYNAMITE™ MAD LIBS® © 2005 Twentieth Century Fox Film Corporation
and Paramount Pictures Corporation. All Rights Reserved. Published by Price Stern Sloan,
a division of Penguin Young Readers Group, 345 Hudson Street, New York, New York 10014.

MAD LIBS® is fun to play with friends, but you can also play it by yourself! To begin with, DO NOT look at the story on the page below. Fill in the blanks on this page with the words called for. Then, using the words you have selected, fill in the blank spaces in the story.

Now you've created your own hilarious MAD LIBS® game!

FASHION 101

NOUN _____

VERB ENDING IN "ING" _____

NOUN _____

ADJECTIVE_____

ADJECTIVE_____

ADJECTIVE_____

NOUN _____

PART OF THE BODY_____

NOUN _____

ADJECTIVE_____

EXCLAMATION_____

NOUN _____

PLURAL NOUN _____

VERB ENDING IN "ING" _____

PLURAL NOUN _____

MAD LIBS
FASHION 101

People were always saying I could be a/an _____ model,

NOUN

but I didn't know a thing about fashion or _____.

VERB ENDING IN "ING"

So in order to bring out my inner _____,

NOUN

I made an appointment with Glamour Shots by Deb. What a/an

_____ experience! She picked out clothing for

ADJECTIVE

my different looks: carefree, serious, and _____. After

ADJECTIVE

dressing me in a/an _____ tube top and placing a/an

ADJECTIVE

_____ in my hair, we went to the set. She placed my

NOUN

arm under my _____ and told me to imagine

PART OF THE BODY

myself in the _____ surrounded by _____

NOUN · ADJECTIVE

sea horses. "_____!" she said. "Are you sure you've

EXCLAMATION

never done this before? You're an absolute _____!"

NOUN

Once my _____ are developed, I'm planning to

PLURAL NOUN

submit them to several _____ agencies, and

VERB ENDING IN "ING"

Napoleon's uncle Rico said he'd love to be my manager! Hollywood

_____, here I come!

PLURAL NOUN

From NAPOLEON DYNAMITE™ MAD LIBS® © 2005 Twentieth Century Fox Film Corporation
and Paramount Pictures Corporation. All Rights Reserved. Published by Price Stern Sloan,
a division of Penguin Young Readers Group, 345 Hudson Street, New York, New York 10014.

MAD LIBS® is fun to play with friends, but you can also play it by yourself! To begin with, DO NOT look at the story on the page below. Fill in the blanks on this page with the words called for. Then, using the words you have selected, fill in the blank spaces in the story.

Now you've created your own hilarious MAD LIBS® game!

NAPOLEON'S BROTHER, KIP

PERSON IN ROOM (MALE)_____

NOUN _____

NUMBER _____

NOUN _____

EXCLAMATION_____

ADJECTIVE_____

ADJECTIVE_____

PLURAL NOUN _____

PLURAL NOUN _____

NOUN _____

PLURAL NOUN _____

PLURAL NOUN _____

NOUN _____

VERB ENDING IN "ING" _____

COUNTRY _____

NAME OF READER _____

MAD LIBS
NAPOLEON'S BROTHER, KIP

I'm so jealous of my cousin, _____. He's a real

PERSON IN ROOM (MALE)

_____-magnet, just like Napoleon Dynamite's brother,

NOUN

Kip. So when a CD arrived in the mail awarding me _____

NUMBER

free hours on the inter_____, I thought, "_____!

NOUN   EXCLAMATION

This is my big chance!" I registered and created a/an _____

ADJECTIVE

profile. I said I was _____-looking, into exercise and

ADJECTIVE

_____, and seeking some cool _____

PLURAL NOUN   PLURAL NOUN

to chat with. I guess my _____ impressed them because as

NOUN

soon as I entered the _____ chat room, I was bombarded

PLURAL NOUN

with instant _____, and they all wanted to chat with

PLURAL NOUN

me! A few of them asked me for my _____, and if I

NOUN

wanted to go _____. Ever since I joined

VERB ENDING IN "ING"

_____ Online, the girls go crazy about the

COUNTRY

_____-meister!

NAME OF READER

From NAPOLEON DYNAMITE™ MAD LIBS® © 2005 Twentieth Century Fox Film Corporation and Paramount Pictures Corporation. All Rights Reserved. Published by Price Stern Sloan, a division of Penguin Young Readers Group, 345 Hudson Street, New York, New York 10014.

MAD LIBS® is fun to play with friends, but you can also play it by yourself! To begin with, DO NOT look at the story on the page below. Fill in the blanks on this page with the words called for. Then, using the words you have selected, fill in the blank spaces in the story.

Now you've created your own hilarious MAD LIBS® game!

GLAMOUR SHOTS BY DEB

NOUN _____

ADVERB_____

PLURAL NOUN _____

NOUN _____

ADJECTIVE_____

ADJECTIVE_____

PLURAL NOUN _____

ADJECTIVE_____

ADJECTIVE_____

NOUN _____

NOUN _____

NOUN _____

ADJECTIVE_____

ADJECTIVE_____

NOUN _____

NOUN _____

ADJECTIVE_____

ADJECTIVE_____

MAD LIBS
GLAMOUR SHOTS BY DEB

Do you want to look like a/an _____ star? Do people

            NOUN

_____ tell you that you ought to be in _____

   ADVERB   PLURAL NOUN

and have your _____ up in lights? Well, you're in luck. For

             NOUN

a limited time, Glamour Shots by Deb is giving a/an _____

                                        ADJECTIVE

75 percent discount. Deb will take special care to make you look

really _____. There's no need to bring your own makeup

      ADJECTIVE

or changes of _____. Deb has a/an _____

            PLURAL NOUN   ADJECTIVE

line for you to pick from. And there's no travel involved. Deb has a

variety of _____ backdrops that will put you in a wild

             ADJECTIVE

_____ or on a serene _____-top, even in a/an

   NOUN   NOUN

_____ on the Riviera. Deb's _____ photos allow you

   NOUN   ADJECTIVE

to preserve a/an _____ moment forever or create a stunning

            ADJECTIVE

_____ memory for that special _____. Whatever

   NOUN   NOUN

your needs, when you think of the best in _____ photography,

                                  ADJECTIVE

think of Glamour Shots by Deb! And if this sounds like a/an

_____ TV commercial, it probably is!

  ADJECTIVE

From NAPOLEON DYNAMITE™ MAD LIBS® © 2005 Twentieth Century Fox Film Corporation
and Paramount Pictures Corporation. All Rights Reserved. Published by Price Stern Sloan,
a division of Penguin Young Readers Group, 345 Hudson Street, New York, New York 10014.

MAD LIBS® is fun to play with friends, but you can also play it by yourself! To begin with, DO NOT look at the story on the page below. Fill in the blanks on this page with the words called for. Then, using the words you have selected, fill in the blank spaces in the story.

Now you've created your own hilarious MAD LIBS® game!

KILLER TETHERBALL TACTICS

ADVERB_____

PART OF THE BODY _____

NOUN _____

VERB ENDING IN "ING" _____

NOUN _____

PART OF THE BODY _____

NOUN _____

PART OF THE BODY _____

NOUN _____

ADJECTIVE_____

MAD LIBS
KILLER TETHERBALL TACTICS

To win at tetherball, it's not enough to be strong physically. You've

also got to be strong _____ . Before the game, you
                        ADVERB

have to look your opponent in the _____ and let him
                                   PART OF THE BODY

know you intend to crush him like a/an _____ . When
                                         NOUN

play begins, you must use Zen _____ techniques such
                                VERB ENDING IN "ING"

as shouting "_____!" every time you hit the ball. This
              NOUN

will force the breath to come from your _____ and
                                         PART OF THE BODY

thus conserve your _____ . As play builds into a
                    NOUN

rhythm, you will establish a pattern by hitting the ball continually

with your left _____ . Then suddenly, when the
                PART OF THE BODY

opposing _____ least expects it, you will switch to
          NOUN

the right! He will be so dazed and confused by this _____
                                                     ADJECTIVE

misdirection that you'll win the game—and probably ruin his life!

From NAPOLEON DYNAMITE™ MAD LIBS® © 2005 Twentieth Century Fox Film Corporation
and Paramount Pictures Corporation. All Rights Reserved. Published by Price Stern Sloan,
a division of Penguin Young Readers Group, 345 Hudson Street, New York, New York 10014.

MAD LIBS® is fun to play with friends, but you can also play it by yourself! To begin with, DO NOT look at the story on the page below. Fill in the blanks on this page with the words called for. Then, using the words you have selected, fill in the blank spaces in the story.

Now you've created your own hilarious MAD LIBS® game!

UNCLE RICO

NOUN _____

NOUN _____

PERSON IN ROOM _____

NOUN _____

PLURAL NOUN _____

NOUN _____

ADJECTIVE _____

ADJECTIVE _____

NOUN _____

ADJECTIVE _____

PLURAL NOUN _____

SAME PERSON _____

NOUN _____

NOUN _____

NUMBER _____

PLURAL NOUN _____

MAD LIBS®
UNCLE RICO

Inspired by Napoleon Dynamite's uncle Rico, I decided to go door-

to-_____ selling _____ware. I went to
          NOUN   NOUN

the home of Mrs. _____ and said, "Have I got a/an
                  PERSON IN ROOM

_____ for you!" Then I proceeded to show her my
      NOUN

selection of fine _____. I picked up a small _____
                    PLURAL NOUN   NOUN

and demonstrated how _____ it was. "This is a/an
                          ADJECTIVE

_____-quality _____, ma'am, and for the
      ADJECTIVE   NOUN

_____ price of just nine dollars and ninety-five _____,
  ADJECTIVE   PLURAL NOUN

you can own the whole set!" Unfortunately, Mrs. _____
                                                  SAME PERSON

wasn't interested . . . until I showed her the free _____
                                                      NOUN

that comes with each _____! Then she bought
                          NOUN

_____ pieces! Wow! If this continues, maybe I'll start
    NUMBER

selling more expensive _____!
                          PLURAL NOUN

From NAPOLEON DYNAMITE™ MAD LIBS® © 2005 Twentieth Century Fox Film Corporation
and Paramount Pictures Corporation. All Rights Reserved. Published by Price Stern Sloan,
a division of Penguin Young Readers Group, 345 Hudson Street, New York, New York 10014.

MAD LIBS® is fun to play with friends, but you can also play it by yourself! To begin with, DO NOT look at the story on the page below. Fill in the blanks on this page with the words called for. Then, using the words you have selected, fill in the blank spaces in the story.

Now you've created your own hilarious MAD LIBS® game!

MY PET LLAMA

NOUN _____

NOUN _____

ADJECTIVE _____

VERB ENDING IN "ING" _____

FIRST NAME (FEMALE) _____

PLURAL NOUN _____

VERB _____

ADVERB _____

SAME FIRST NAME _____

ADJECTIVE _____

NOUN _____

PLURAL NOUN _____

NOUN _____

NOUN _____

MAD LIBS
MY PET LLAMA

Almost everybody has either a cat or a/an _____ as a
NOUN

household _____, and I wanted to be different. I wanted
NOUN

something that would show the world how _____ I am.
ADJECTIVE

I wanted a llama—just like Napoleon Dynamite's—so I brought one

home from the _____ farm and named her
VERB ENDING IN "ING"

_____. I gave her lots of _____ to
FIRST NAME (FEMALE)   PLURAL NOUN

eat and plenty of space to _____ in. She seemed to be
VERB

adjusting _____ until . . . well, llamas apparently
ADVERB

establish dominance by spitting, and I guess _____
SAME FIRST NAME

decided to establish dominance all over me! I showered and washed

the _____ stuff off my body and made sure to
ADJECTIVE

shampoo my _____, but I still smelled like wet
NOUN

_____ for days. Needless to say, I returned the
PLURAL NOUN

llama to the _____ dealer, who exchanged it for a
NOUN

flying _____.
NOUN

From NAPOLEON DYNAMITE™ MAD LIBS® © 2005 Twentieth Century Fox Film Corporation
and Paramount Pictures Corporation. All Rights Reserved. Published by Price Stern Sloan,
a division of Penguin Young Readers Group, 345 Hudson Street, New York, New York 10014.

MAD LIBS® is fun to play with friends, but you can also play it by yourself! To begin with, DO NOT look at the story on the page below. Fill in the blanks on this page with the words called for. Then, using the words you have selected, fill in the blank spaces in the story.

Now you've created your own hilarious MAD LIBS® game!

REX KWON DO

NOUN _____

NOUN _____

NOUN _____

VERB ENDING IN "ING" _____

PLURAL NOUN _____

PART OF THE BODY _____

SAME PART OF THE BODY_____

ADJECTIVE_____

NOUN _____

PLURAL NOUN _____

NOUN _____

PART OF THE BODY _____

NOUN _____

ADJECTIVE_____

VERB ENDING IN "ING" _____

MAD LIBS®
REX KWON DO

I signed up because I wanted the strength of a/an _____,
NOUN

the reflexes of a/an _____, and the _____
NOUN   NOUN

of a man. On day one, we hit the ground _____,
VERB ENDING IN "ING"

with an exercise in _____. I blocked a kick with my
PLURAL NOUN

_____, and immediately Rex had me do it again and
PART OF THE BODY

again and again. Eventually my _____ turned black
SAME PART OF THE BODY

and _____ and swelled up like a large _____!
ADJECTIVE   NOUN

Rex said I should expect a few _____ because self-
PLURAL NOUN

defense is no walk in the _____. He told me to keep a
NOUN

stiff upper _____ and keep going. I did, but now my
PART OF THE BODY

whole body feels like it's been hit by a/an _____. I'm
NOUN

actually dreading next week's _____ lesson: defensive
ADJECTIVE

_____!
VERB ENDING IN "ING"

From NAPOLEON DYNAMITE™ MAD LIBS® © 2005 Twentieth Century Fox Film Corporation
and Paramount Pictures Corporation. All Rights Reserved. Published by Price Stern Sloan,
a division of Penguin Young Readers Group, 345 Hudson Street, New York, New York 10014.

MAD LIBS® is fun to play with friends, but you can also play it by yourself! To begin with, DO NOT look at the story on the page below. Fill in the blanks on this page with the words called for. Then, using the words you have selected, fill in the blank spaces in the story.

Now you've created your own hilarious MAD LIBS® game!

HAPPY HANDS

NOUN _____

ADJECTIVE _____

PART OF THE BODY _____

ADJECTIVE _____

ADJECTIVE _____

NOUN _____

ADJECTIVE _____

VERB _____

NOUN _____

LETTER OF THE ALPHABET _____

VERB _____

ADJECTIVE _____

MAD LIBS
HAPPY HANDS

Today in Happy Hands Club we learned how to sing "You Light Up

My _____" in sign language. It was really quite a/an
           NOUN

_____ experience. For the word "you," simply point at
     ADJECTIVE

a person and use appropriate _____ expressions.
                              PART OF THE BODY

To express "light," flick the _____ finger of your
                               ADJECTIVE

_____ hand upward twice so that it thumps (lightly)
   ADJECTIVE

on the underside of your _____ or jaw. The
                              NOUN

_____ sign for "up" is to _____ up. You
    ADJECTIVE   VERB

signify "my" by pointing a/an _____ at yourself. To
                                  NOUN

indicate "life," you sign the letters *L I F* _____.
                                              LETTER OF THE ALPHABET

Congratulations—you just learned how to _____ a/an
                                             VERB

_____ song!
    ADJECTIVE

From NAPOLEON DYNAMITE™ MAD LIBS® © 2005 Twentieth Century Fox Film Corporation
and Paramount Pictures Corporation. All Rights Reserved. Published by Price Stern Sloan,
a division of Penguin Young Readers Group, 345 Hudson Street, New York, New York 10014.

MAD LIBS® is fun to play with friends, but you can also play it by yourself! To begin with, DO NOT look at the story on the page below. Fill in the blanks on this page with the words called for. Then, using the words you have selected, fill in the blank spaces in the story.

Now you've created your own hilarious MAD LIBS® game!

IT'S GOURMET, GOSH!

ADJECTIVE_____

ADJECTIVE_____

NOUN _____

VERB ENDING IN "ING" _____

NOUN _____

PLURAL NOUN _____

NOUN _____

ADVERB_____

NOUN _____

ADJECTIVE_____

ADJECTIVE_____

ADJECTIVE_____

PERSON IN ROOM _____

ADJECTIVE_____

NOUN _____

ADJECTIVE_____

NOUN _____

TYPE OF LIQUID _____

NOUN _____

MAD LIBS
IT'S GOURMET, GOSH!

This recipe for _____ potato casserole provides a
            ADJECTIVE

quick and _____ way to eat Napoleon-style. First,
            ADJECTIVE

preheat your _____ to 375 degrees. Then, coat a glass
            NOUN

dish with _____ spray and spread some ground
       VERB ENDING IN "ING"

_____ over the bottom. Sprinkle diced _____
    NOUN   PLURAL NOUN

on top, followed by grated cheese and cream of _____
                                                  NOUN

soup. Spread _____ with a long _____.
               ADVERB   NOUN

Finally, add the potatoes! Bake for 30 minutes and check that they

aren't turning too _____. They should be nice and
                      ADJECTIVE

_____-looking. (Note: If they appear too _____,
  ADJECTIVE   ADJECTIVE

you can feed this batch to _____!) When the
                            PERSON IN ROOM

casserole is thoroughly _____, you will have a
                            ADJECTIVE

complete meal all in one _____. It should be
                            NOUN

_____ inside, with a crispy _____
   ADJECTIVE   NOUN

crust. Be sure to enjoy it with a glass of _____, and
                                           TYPE OF LIQUID

then for a surprise dessert, serve some _____ cookies.
                                           NOUN

From NAPOLEON DYNAMITE™ MAD LIBS® © 2005 Twentieth Century Fox Film Corporation
and Paramount Pictures Corporation. All Rights Reserved. Published by Price Stern Sloan,
a division of Penguin Young Readers Group, 345 Hudson Street, New York, New York 10014.

MAD LIBS® is fun to play with friends, but you can also play it by yourself! To begin with, DO NOT look at the story on the page below. Fill in the blanks on this page with the words called for. Then, using the words you have selected, fill in the blank spaces in the story.

Now you've created your own hilarious MAD LIBS® game!

NAPOLEON THE ARTIST

PLURAL NOUN _____

ADJECTIVE _____

PERSON IN ROOM _____

ADJECTIVE _____

NOUN _____

PLURAL NOUN _____

PART OF THE BODY _____

PLURAL NOUN _____

PLURAL NOUN _____

PLURAL NOUN _____

VERB ENDING IN "ING" _____

ADJECTIVE _____

ADJECTIVE _____

VERB _____

Ladies and _____, we are here today to unveil the

PLURAL NOUN

most recent portrait completed by the _____artist

ADJECTIVE

Napoleon Dynamite. Titled simply, "_____," the

PERSON IN ROOM

subject of this portrait is both _____ and menacing.

ADJECTIVE

He/She has a/an _____ quality that asks us to

NOUN

seriously consider our own personal _____. Notice

PLURAL NOUN

the unnaturally elongated _____, suggesting the artist

PART OF THE BODY

may have a preoccupation with spiritual _____.

PLURAL NOUN

Mr. Dynamite's use of line encourages the exploration of new

_____, while the lack of other _____

PLURAL NOUN   PLURAL NOUN

undermines the substructure of critical _____.

VERB ENDING IN "ING"

He is a master of detail; it must have taken three hours to get the

_____ shading on the upper lip and the _____

ADJECTIVE   ADJECTIVE

cheeks. This drawing makes one want to _____with

VERB

reckless abandon.

From NAPOLEON DYNAMITE™ MAD LIBS® © 2005 Twentieth Century Fox Film Corporation
and Paramount Pictures Corporation. All Rights Reserved. Published by Price Stern Sloan,
a division of Penguin Young Readers Group, 345 Hudson Street, New York, New York 10014.

MAD LIBS® is fun to play with friends, but you can also play it by yourself! To begin with, DO NOT look at the story on the page below. Fill in the blanks on this page with the words called for. Then, using the words you have selected, fill in the blank spaces in the story.

Now you've created your own hilarious MAD LIBS® game!

THE SCHOOL DANCE

PLURAL NOUN _____

NOUN _____

NOUN _____

PLURAL NOUN _____

ADJECTIVE _____

NOUN _____

NOUN _____

PLURAL NOUN _____

PLURAL NOUN _____

TYPE OF LIQUID _____

NOUN _____

ADJECTIVE _____

ADVERB _____

ADJECTIVE _____

SAME ADJECTIVE _____

NOUN _____

PLURAL NOUN _____

MAD LIBS®
THE SCHOOL DANCE

Ah, the old school dance! Some _____ never change.

PLURAL NOUN

The _____ committee decorates the _____

NOUN   NOUN

with streamers and _____, trying to make it look

PLURAL NOUN

really _____ ,or maybe like a tropical _____.

ADJECTIVE   NOUN

A disc jockey or musical _____ spins rockin' _____,

NOUN   PLURAL NOUN

and a few older _____ are invited to chaperone. You

PLURAL NOUN

can always count on someone to pour _____ into the

TYPE OF LIQUID

punch bowl when the _____ isn't looking, and for some

NOUN

_____ freshman to get _____ sick. The

ADJECTIVE   ADVERB

popular kids don't even attend because they consider dances to be

" _____ ," and others come but leave quickly because,

ADJECTIVE

again, "those things are _____." The best part is watching

SAME ADJECTIVE

everyone try to get a/an _____ for the dance, then, once

NOUN

it starts, they split up and hang out with their usual _____

PLURAL NOUN

anyway.

From NAPOLEON DYNAMITE™ MAD LIBS® © 2005 Twentieth Century Fox Film Corporation and Paramount Pictures Corporation. All Rights Reserved. Published by Price Stern Sloan, a division of Penguin Young Readers Group, 345 Hudson Street, New York, New York 10014.

MAD LIBS® is fun to play with friends, but you can also play it by yourself! To begin with, DO NOT look at the story on the page below. Fill in the blanks on this page with the words called for. Then, using the words you have selected, fill in the blank spaces in the story.

Now you've created your own hilarious MAD LIBS® game!

PEDRO FOR PRESIDENT

NOUN _____

VERB _____

PLURAL NOUN _____

PLURAL NOUN _____

PLURAL NOUN _____

PLURAL NOUN _____

NOUN _____

ADJECTIVE _____

NOUN _____

ADJECTIVE _____

PERSON IN ROOM _____

NOUN _____

NOUN _____

PLURAL NOUN _____

MAD LIBS
PEDRO FOR PRESIDENT

I want to run for school _____, but I have no idea

NOUN

how to _____ a campaign. Pedro handed out

VERB

boondoggle _____ and hung "Vote for Pedro"

PLURAL NOUN

_____ on the walls. Maybe I should hand out

PLURAL NOUN

boondoggle _____ and hang my own _____.

PLURAL NOUN ... PLURAL NOUN

Pedro offered everyone his protection. Maybe I should offer everyone

my _____. Pedro made a piñata that looked like Summer, his

NOUN

_____ opponent. Maybe I should make a/an _____

ADJECTIVE ... NOUN

in the shape of my _____ opponent, _____.

ADJECTIVE ... PERSON IN ROOM

But if I do everything Pedro did, people will call me a copy-

_____. Maybe I should just say that if they vote for me

NOUN

I'll get a/an _____ machine for the cafeteria and

NOUN

try to foster better student/teacher _____. Yeah, that's

PLURAL NOUN

pretty original!

From NAPOLEON DYNAMITE™ MAD LIBS® © 2005 Twentieth Century Fox Film Corporation
and Paramount Pictures Corporation. All Rights Reserved. Published by Price Stern Sloan,
a division of Penguin Young Readers Group, 345 Hudson Street, New York, New York 10014.

MAD LIBS® is fun to play with friends, but you can also play it by yourself! To begin with, DO NOT look at the story on the page below. Fill in the blanks on this page with the words called for. Then, using the words you have selected, fill in the blank spaces in the story.

Now you've created your own hilarious MAD LIBS® game!

DYNAMITE DANCE MOVES

PLURAL NOUN _____

ADJECTIVE_____

VERB _____

PLURAL NOUN _____

NOUN _____

ADJECTIVE_____

NOUN _____

ADVERB_____

NOUN _____

NOUN _____

PLURAL NOUN _____

ADJECTIVE_____

PLURAL NOUN _____

NOUN _____

PLURAL NOUN _____

NOUN _____

ADVERB_____

VERB _____

MAD LIBS
DYNAMITE DANCE MOVES

In my thirty-year career as a critic of performing _____,
                                                    PLURAL NOUN

I have never come across a more _____ dancer than
                                  ADJECTIVE

Napoleon Dynamite. To watch him _____ is to be
                                  VERB

reminded of humanity's wild _____ and deep-seated
                             PLURAL NOUN

yearning for an unattainable _____. His performance
                              NOUN

following Pedro's _____ campaign speech was unlike
                   ADJECTIVE

any _____ work I have ever seen. He moved
     NOUN

_____, as if there were a/an _____
ADVERB   NOUN

running through his _____, trying to get out. How
                     NOUN

this young man expressed the dreams and _____ of
                                          PLURAL NOUN

an entire school of teenagers is truly _____. He
                                        ADJECTIVE

understood their hopes and _____. He felt their every
                            PLURAL NOUN

_____, and he used _____-like
NOUN   PLURAL NOUN

movements and _____-esque music to demonstrate
                NOUN

it. He delivered his message _____ and, in a word, that
                              ADVERB

message was, "_____."
               VERB

From NAPOLEON DYNAMITE™ MAD LIBS® © 2005 Twentieth Century Fox Film Corporation
and Paramount Pictures Corporation. All Rights Reserved. Published by Price Stern Sloan,
a division of Penguin Young Readers Group, 345 Hudson Street, New York, New York 10014.

MAD LIBS® is fun to play with friends, but you can also play it by yourself! To begin with, DO NOT look at the story on the page below. Fill in the blanks on this page with the words called for. Then, using the words you have selected, fill in the blank spaces in the story.

Now you've created your own hilarious MAD LIBS® game!

MY DATE

NOUN _____

PERSON IN ROOM _____

NOUN _____

ADJECTIVE_____

NOUN _____

NOUN _____

NOUN _____

ADJECTIVE_____

ADJECTIVE_____

ADVERB_____

NOUN _____

ADJECTIVE_____

PLURAL NOUN _____

NOUN _____

NOUN _____

ADJECTIVE_____

MAD LIBS
MY DATE

I didn't want to go to a/an _____ dance with
NOUN

_____, but my mom said she'd take away my
PERSON IN ROOM

_____ privileges for a week if I didn't. So he picked
NOUN

me up wearing a/an _____ suit that looked like it
ADJECTIVE

came from a secondhand-_____ store. We got off on
NOUN

the wrong _____ the minute he stepped into my
NOUN

_____ and handed me a/an _____
NOUN   ADJECTIVE

drawing. I tried to be polite and said, "Oh, what a/an _____
ADJECTIVE

flower." He stared at me _____ and said, "It's you in
ADVERB

your cheerleading _____." From there, things went
NOUN

from bad to _____. At the dance, he didn't say more
ADJECTIVE

than two _____ to me all night. I even had to get my
PLURAL NOUN

own _____ from the _____ bowl! Next
NOUN   NOUN

time I'd rather lose the _____ privileges!
ADJECTIVE

From NAPOLEON DYNAMITE™ MAD LIBS® © 2005 Twentieth Century Fox Film Corporation
and Paramount Pictures Corporation. All Rights Reserved. Published by Price Stern Sloan,
a division of Penguin Young Readers Group, 345 Hudson Street, New York, New York 10014.

MAD LIBS® is fun to play with friends, but you can also play it by yourself! To begin with, DO NOT look at the story on the page below. Fill in the blanks on this page with the words called for. Then, using the words you have selected, fill in the blank spaces in the story.

Now you've created your own hilarious MAD LIBS® game!

MY BEST FRIEND

PERSON IN ROOM _____

PLURAL NOUN _____

VERB _____

PLURAL NOUN _____

NOUN _____

SAME PERSON _____

PLURAL NOUN _____

ADJECTIVE _____

NOUN _____

NOUN _____

SAME PERSON _____

NOUN _____

ADJECTIVE _____

NOUN _____

PLURAL NOUN _____

PART OF THE BODY _____

PLURAL NOUN _____

MAD LIBS

MY BEST FRIEND

Just like Napoleon and Pedro, my best friend, _____,
                                              PERSON IN ROOM

and I go together like meat and _____. We
                                 PLURAL NOUN

_____ together at school; we ride _____
VERB   PLURAL NOUN

around town, and help each other with our _____-
                                           NOUN

work. Not only that, but _____ also offers me his/her
                         SAME PERSON

protection. For example, I was recently riding my bike over some

very rough _____ near a/an _____
           PLURAL NOUN   ADJECTIVE

ravine. I hit one particularly bad _____ and went
                                   NOUN

flying in the _____. _____ jumped off
              NOUN   SAME PERSON

his/her _____ and caught me before I could fall off
        NOUN

the _____ cliff. No one had ever risked his/her
    ADJECTIVE

_____ to save me like that before. I guess that's what
NOUN

good _____ are for. You stick your
     PLURAL NOUN

_____ out for each other no matter what the
PART OF THE BODY

_____ are!
PLURAL NOUN

From NAPOLEON DYNAMITE™ MAD LIBS® © 2005 Twentieth Century Fox Film Corporation
and Paramount Pictures Corporation. All Rights Reserved. Published by Price Stern Sloan,
a division of Penguin Young Readers Group, 345 Hudson Street, New York, New York 10014.

MAD LIBS® is fun to play with friends, but you can also play it by yourself! To begin with, DO NOT look at the story on the page below. Fill in the blanks on this page with the words called for. Then, using the words you have selected, fill in the blank spaces in the story.

Now you've created your own hilarious MAD LIBS® game!

MYTHICAL CREATURE

NOUN _____

NOUN _____

SILLY WORD _____

NOUN _____

NOUN _____

NOUN _____

ADJECTIVE _____

NOUN _____

VERB _____

PLURAL NOUN _____

PART OF THE BODY _____

VERB _____

NOUN _____

SAME SILLY WORD _____

PLURAL NOUN _____

PART OF THE BODY _____

PLURAL NOUN _____

NOUN _____

MAD LIBS
MYTHICAL CREATURE

The liger may be Napoleon's favorite large _____, but
_____NOUN

it's nothing in size and _____ compared to the
_____NOUN

_____, which is a cross between a/an _____
SILLY WORD   NOUN

and a/an _____. This ferocious _____ is
_____NOUN   NOUN

the most _____ creature in the _____
_____ADJECTIVE   NOUN

kingdom. Its skills are far superior to the liger's. It has the power to

_____ at lightning speeds and believe it or not, to
VERB

read people's inner _____. But remember this: You
_____PLURAL NOUN

should never stare directly at this creature's _____ or
_____PART OF THE BODY

_____ anywhere near it. That is considered a/an _____
VERB   NOUN

of aggression. The _____ can be tamed, however, and
_____SAME SILLY WORD

can protect you from wild _____. And just like a man, the
_____PLURAL NOUN

way to its heart is through its _____. So, if you just provide
_____PART OF THE BODY

a few _____ at mealtime, you will have a/an _____
____PLURAL NOUN   NOUN

for life!

From NAPOLEON DYNAMITE™ MAD LIBS® © 2005 Twentieth Century Fox Film Corporation
and Paramount Pictures Corporation. All Rights Reserved. Published by Price Stern Sloan,
a division of Penguin Young Readers Group, 345 Hudson Street, New York, New York 10014.

MAD LIBS® is fun to play with friends, but you can also play it by yourself! To begin with, DO NOT look at the story on the page below. Fill in the blanks on this page with the words called for. Then, using the words you have selected, fill in the blank spaces in the story.

Now you've created your own hilarious MAD LIBS® game!

ASK NAPOLEON DYNAMITE

NOUN _____

ADJECTIVE _____

ADVERB _____

ADJECTIVE _____

PLURAL NOUN _____

PERSON IN ROOM _____

NOUN _____

NOUN _____

ADJECTIVE _____

NOUN _____

ADJECTIVE _____

NOUN _____

NOUN _____

ADJECTIVE _____

MAD LIBS
ASK NAPOLEON DYNAMITE

Whenever I have _____ problems and life begins to
            NOUN

make me _____, I just say: "What would Napoleon
        ADJECTIVE

Dynamite do?" and then I _____ start to feel _____.
                        ADVERB   ADJECTIVE

For example, I asked my best _____ if I should invite
                            PLURAL NOUN

_____ to the school _____. He/She said, "No
PERSON IN ROOM   NOUN

way," because she'd never be seen with a/an _____
                                                        NOUN

like me. I felt so _____, I was ready to throw in the
                    ADJECTIVE

_____. Then I imagined Napoleon's shining red hair
        NOUN

and _____ face uttering these inspiring words: "Heck,
        ADJECTIVE

yeah!" and I swallowed my _____ and decided to ask her
                            NOUN

anyway. Her answer was no, but the point is that I faced my

_____ and conquered it. With Napoleon as my guide, I
        NOUN

hope to have _____ experiences like this all the time!
                ADJECTIVE

From NAPOLEON DYNAMITE™ MAD LIBS® © 2005 Twentieth Century Fox Film Corporation
and Paramount Pictures Corporation. All Rights Reserved. Published by Price Stern Sloan,
a division of Penguin Young Readers Group, 345 Hudson Street, New York, New York 10014.

MAD LIBS® is fun to play with friends, but you can also play it by yourself! To begin with, DO NOT look at the story on the page below. Fill in the blanks on this page with the words called for. Then, using the words you have selected, fill in the blank spaces in the story.

Now you've created your own hilarious MAD LIBS® game!

LOVE LETTER

ADJECTIVE _____

NOUN _____

ARTICLE OF CLOTHING (PLURAL) _____

ADJECTIVE _____

PART OF THE BODY _____

PLURAL NOUN _____

NOUN _____

ADJECTIVE _____

PLURAL NOUN _____

NOUN _____

PLURAL NOUN _____

NOUN _____

LAST NAME _____

ADJECTIVE _____

ADVERB _____

PERSON IN ROOM _____

MAD LIBS
LOVE LETTER

Dear Napoleon Dynamite,

I think you're the most _____ boy in the whole
                              ADJECTIVE

_____. Your Hammer _____ and
      NOUN   ARTICLE OF CLOTHING (PLURAL)

_____ moon boots make my _____ go
      ADJECTIVE   PART OF THE BODY

pitter-pat. I wish I could tell you in person, but every time I'm near

you, I feel _____ in my stomach and I can't open my
                 PLURAL NOUN

_____. I heard you hunted wolverines last summer.
      NOUN

How _____! I also heard you like dresses with puffy
         ADJECTIVE

_____. I have one, and I'll wear it next week at the
     PLURAL NOUN

_____ party if you'll go with me. We can just go as
      NOUN

_____ if you want—no pressure. I have to go now—
    PLURAL NOUN

I'm late for _____ class and Mrs. _____ hates
                  NOUN   LAST NAME

me. Hoping for a/an _____ response . . .
                         ADJECTIVE

_____ yours,
      ADVERB

_____
   PERSON IN ROOM

From NAPOLEON DYNAMITE™ MAD LIBS® © 2005 Twentieth Century Fox Film Corporation
and Paramount Pictures Corporation. All Rights Reserved. Published by Price Stern Sloan,
a division of Penguin Young Readers Group, 345 Hudson Street, New York, New York 10014.

This book is published by

PSS!
PRICE STERN SLOAN
whose other splendid titles include such literary classics as

The Original #1 Mad Libs®

Son of Mad Libs®

Nancy Drew® Mad Libs®

Vacation Fun Mad Libs®

Winter Games Mad Libs®

Christmas Fun Mad Libs®

Graduation Mad Libs®

Betty and Veronica® Mad Libs®

The Apprentice™ Mad Libs®

The Powerpuff Girls™ Mad Libs®

Shrek™ Mad Libs®

Shrek 2™ Mad Libs®

Scooby-Doo!™ Halloween Mad Libs®

Scooby-Doo!™ Mystery Mad Libs®

Scooby-Doo!™ Movie Mad Libs®

Scooby-Doo!™ 2 Monsters Unleashed Mad Libs®

Catwoman™ Mad Libs®

Teen Titans™ Mad Libs®

Guinness World Records™ Mad Libs®

The Mad Libs® Worst-Case Scenario™ Survival Handbook

The Mad Libs® Worst-Case Scenario™ Survival Handbook 2

The Mad Libs® Worst-Case Scenario™ Survival Handbook: Travel

The Mad Libs® Worst-Case Scenario™ Survival Handbook: Holidays

Fear Factor™ Mad Libs®

Fear Factor™ Mad Libs®: Ultimate Gross Out!

Survivor™ Mad Libs®

and many, many more!
Mad Libs® are available wherever books are sold.